Make It Yours

Sandy Lee Carlson

Presentation by *BookLeaf Publishing*

Web: www.bookleafpub.com

E-mail: info@bookleafpub.com

ISBN: 9789357696388

First edition 2023

DEDICATION

For Adella, the joy of my life and a living song

PREFACE

Thank you for picking up this book, which is the product of years of living in Connecticut, close to the landscape, close to family, and, always, close to the bone. "Close to the bone" is a defining aspect of being a New Englander; we say what we mean, honoring the truth of genuine experience. While no offence is intended, we take the risk of offending in the interest of being accurate, honest, and truthful. Nowadays, young people say "I'm being real with you" as if this were a special moment worthy of note. In the time and place from which I write, it is a given, a fundamental of integrity. The point? No matter how you feel about the person you are dealing with, you, at the very least, know who they are. For real. Welcome to Connecticut. How long will you stay?

I Stay

I step forward, you step back
Forward and back again
You lift your nose
And roll your neck
Your young behind you
Following your lead
Into and out of the woods.
There is your vulnerability
On full display:
Your hungry cubs and your
Walking the line between the material world
And the fine line between garbage and fear
You do not trust us anywhere near your children
Though it seems also you would have us do
something.
Stay there, the dance says. So it goes.
I stay.

Too Late

Becoming my mother,
I have taken the two-week-old
Stephanotis and trimmed the stems
And returned them to the vase
Where they started
Their blossoming, their heads
Resting at the top of the vase
Like swimmers resting their little heads
On the edge of the pool
After a keen race.
Mom could make them last.
The color mattered. The gift. The love.
The gift of her daughter.
Dad wouldn't, maybe couldn't, add water.
He never asked for help
But lamented how fast flowers die.
He ignored what mom knew: ask for water,
Honor the gift.
It was too late.

Learning to Ride

I remember my first time on a horse,
My mother watching from outside the ring
As I put my right foot in the stirrup
And hauled myself up,
Swinging my left leg over the animal
And slipping my left foot safely into the stirrup.
She was an old mare well used to children
Who had no idea about horse power.
She carried me around the ring,
Giving me time to learn to move with her easy gait.
My instructor told me to sit tall,
To roll with her moves,
To hold the reins in my right hand,
Rest my left hand on my thigh–
But mostly to sit tall.
The horse is not a chair, not a couch.
You are a guest. Let Pegasus fly.
My mother watched
As I learned to trot and to canter,
As I sought the rhythm of this matriarch.
There would be no race, no finish line
In my time of riding horses.
Instead, I learned to sit properly
To read the gestures of a mother
Who has done it all before
And would get me home
Better versed in
Knowing my place.

Night

Red-tailed hawk
Calls into the grey air
A silent owl
Glides into oncoming dark
Wood ducks slip
Behind Canada geese
In the icing winter pond
What remains of light
Freezes into the ice.
Small birds, in silhouette,
Flit amid the brambles.
I am there, too--
Wingless, reduced to shadow,
Becoming one with the night.

Cutting Back

I thought of cutting back the bushes
To impose order on summer's chaos
And fool myself into believing I have
Something to do with how things are.

I studied the branches to decide
Which ones I might eliminate.

Despite August dryness, the bushes are lush.
The rhododendron carries the promise of next May's
bouquets
And is full of tufted titmice waiting
Their turn at the feeder and at the bath.
So, too, is the forsythia full with leaves now.
From within, the sparrows watch squirrels
Launch themselves into the woods from the bushes.
The cardinals fly in and out, as well,
Drying themselves in safety after a short dip.
The branches make the hawks' life
That bit more challenging.
There is safety in this sprawl.

My neighbor says my gardens
Are overgrown, but in a good way.
This is a true and happy fact, though he
Doesn't quite know what he means. He has never
Shared his opinion with me seated here

Beside me, where he might quietly watch the birds
Feast and bathe and lift themselves up, up, up
The laddered branches of the white pine,
All the while filling silence with song.
I will invite him
After I do not cut back the bushes.
They are home, and this is how it is
In a good way.

Nipping Life in the Bud

The orange-plate special
Would be adorned with a garnish
Of home grown lettuce
If it weren't for you and your conniving ways
Stalking the garden before dawn,
Feasting on romaine and bib and Boston,
Nipping life in the bud of salad dreams.

What to do with you?
Musings in the email thread
To erstwhile gardeners
Range from showing understanding to a nursing
mother
To eradicating you. Period. Case closed.

A cranky voice, mine, adds coarse language
To the conversation:
To heck with you and your lettuce, you who become
warriors
Over $1.29 in lettuce seeds you grew yourself
In your battle against pandemic boredom.
A hungry mother ate your leaves and so fed her
young.
This is a problem because you are now starving?

Welcome to the wilderness,
You who cannot tell a bear from a deer
But fear both if they come too close
To your idea of yourself
As someone who can cope with the unknown.

Meet the nursing mother
Who ate your lettuce.
Meet her young, whom you nourished
With your pandemic hobby.

Stand still and look
At her swollen teats and growing offspring
At her big eyes that would make sense of you.
Look at grace embodied, fueled on your leaves.
Look how they become invisible right in front of you.
They are part of the landscape. Know it.
Silence your mind long enough to recognize a
miracle.
Stalking the garden before dawn,
Feasting on romaine and bib and Boston,
Nipping life in the bud of salad dreams.

Think: What is the problem you would solve,
And whose is it?

Squash Bugs

Is this a private fight,
Or can anyone join?
I think to myself
As I do not wait for an answer
But use the dogs' as-yet empty
Poop bag to pinch the life
Out of a bug preparing
To suck the life out of the leaves
Of my squash plants
While his dutiful wife
Lays eggs on the undersides
Of leaves whose fullness creates shade
For squash and keep the ground moist.
These winged monsters the color of sterile earth
Gorge themselves:
Simple New England vegetables
That are bland
And therefore fit in with everybody
On your spice rack
Drained dry by an invader
And his family of monsters.

This is not a fight
But a war, I say to myself
As I discover a battalion of beetles
Swarming the leaves
As I recall with fondness
A friend no longer suffering

Who once said of mosquitoes
If you don't kill them,
They will get you.
It's not about being nice,
Living and let live.
It's about survival.
My friend was an advocate
Of brute force.
All of his enemies were on the scale of Putin.
They understood, and that made it fair.
So, therefore, could a proper battle
Ensue
That we might regain our
Squash.

In this battle,
My friend, once a marine, speaks to my soul.
I hate parasites.
I pinch the life out of bugs,
And when I hear they do not like dill,
I take what dill I have
For my potato-leek soup
And sprinkle it on the leaves
Of my squash.
I shake cayenne pepper
All over the garden,
Also to protect my squash.

Eventually, I win the war
Though summer is over
And the bugs have packed it in.
The squash came and came.

We took pictures of the flowers.
We ate. We taught the lesson
And we learned it:
Take care of what you love.
Give it everything.

The Fit

Spend some time turning
The pieces around in your mind:
They find their fit
Even that odd shape
Its sharp edges
Slicing your heart
Like a lump of veal
The plaintive calf cry
Bleating beating
Defeating your heart
The light dawns
And you see
A key,
Not a knife,
A door opening:
"Your daughter called
To see how you made out.
She said to say she loves you."
A successful operation
A robust recovery
For a few hours
Then a sudden decline
Slow passing

Not alone but admitted,
Home again.
At peace
In the interlacing constellations
Of memory
Raised up, alight, a light,
Home again
Alive at heart,
My heart.
I have held this piece a long time
Endured the lacerations
Because I have loved you,
Dad.
I have been
Waiting, waiting, waiting
For time to make the fit.

Domestic Life

My call
Stopped him
Saved her, maybe
She always went back
To the living room
The noise
The man she loved.

I had my water.
I would be OK.
Everything is OK,
She would say,
And I would lose all sense
Of time
Amid lies.
She loved me
And tried to hold it together.

That was the best she could do.

He yelled and slammed and hovered
Until she said those magic words:

I'm sorry.

And then silence came

And I would listen for two sets of footsteps,
Retreating voices
Remembering the children are asleep,
Bathroom noises, box-spring noises--

Clues she was alive.

In the morning
She would say
I love you, honey,
As he left for work.

I would know then: she survived.
I lived it again:
The pain the fear
The loud noise yelling

Mom, I call.
Come to me!
She comes
And I imagine her
A skeleton, the walking dead
A tattered life.
I am three, I know cartoons
And TV shows with magic and witchcraft:
A tattered life I can imagine.

I need a drink of water.
Stripped of life,
My mother responds to my call.

As I stop the noise
For a moment
My father
Her drunk husband
Fills the air with threats
And the unimaginable.

Look at the pictures from back then and see
How she ages in just a few years
(She would blame us later; she had to.)

I am three, like I said.
Then four, five, six, seven….

Here I am now.
Fifty-three
They are gone,
Yet I can't stop wondering
If she will make it.

Archetype

"It seems, as one becomes older
That the past has another pattern
And ceases to be a mere sequence,"

So it seems tumbling through time
To Grendel's lair, where the deep fear
Of patternmakers keeps him home days

Until chaos intrudes on gold-gathering
A night battle, brutality, lost arms
And a mother who would have the last word

Home is home and who belongs where
I would fight to the end for you, fight to know
Where you are, to find you here

I go back through ghost stories
To Odysseus in the underworld
Searching in the dark of memory

For Mother's love become spirit
So strong he saw her, heard her, followed her word
Went home like a ghost as if for the first time

Heartache heartbreak, broken heart
You are the star of her universe
She would have you burn bright.

I go back again to the first story
A Mother's blessing, a deep dive, a search for
eternity
Go back, you fool, find it where you began

Dig deep in the sand, unearth the pattern of time
This dazzling eternal moment is your to find.
Dance to the beat of your own wild pulse.

Go.
Go home.
Stop breaking my heart.

Dear One

On a knoll
A hind
Watching
Curious
Walking toward us
No fear
Closer and closer and closer
Follows us into the woods
Watching
Closer and closer
Cool gray morning
Quiet
A blue jay chimes the hour
Throaty bell calling the day
Quiet steps
No broken branches
Following
On the soft ground
Soft eyes
Unblinking, wide
Spirit made visible
You watch
You are seen
You let us go
You watch
You follow
Sure and warm

Wooden Bowl

"Two dollars" in pencil on the Mohegan Trail
For a wooden bowl, one fluid scuplted curve of
Something hard (maple or birch or ash).
My grandmother nicked and scraped it over years
With the steel vegetable chopper her grandfather
Fashioned from a spade.
She scraped, scraped, scraped, scraped, scraped
Maine into soups, stews. "Two dollars" in pencil,
Clear after 20 years' use and 17 in a
Cardboard box under crumpled bits of newspaper
Coated yet with the tallow of broiled steaks and
chops.
My grandmother kept the bowl near the gas stove
With its broiler, well, four burners, two ovens.
That was her mother's stove, cast iron, still working
Somewhere even now. They were proud of it,
What you can keep if you take care over time.
There is nothing like a well-seasoned gas stove.
I smell ancient dinners in the newspaper.
Then, I press the paper into a loose ball,
Toss it aside,
And put in twelve new Macintosh apples,
Grown local.

Seagull Memory

Seagulls sit
On the shore and wait for the tide
To wash them away
When they are ready
To die.

My father told me so
Long, long ago.

That is why you see them
Looking left and right crouched
In the sun,
And all the while the tide creeps in
And strokes with a gentle monotony
Against the puffed up and gleaming chests
Of very old seagulls.

It is a decent thing,
To know when to die.

It's easy to forget this
About seagulls
When they are swooping and screaming
Above our mountains of rubbish,
Indignant, perhaps,

At what the hunt has become.

But seagulls know.
They die listening to the ocean
Pulling against the stones on the beach.
The steady chiming on the wet pebbles
Is enough,

And the clanging of rigging and masts
Like taps
On the breeze.

Dad Nods to the Nest

Greens the ospreys
Added to their nest
Have managed to grow.

Our ospreys have gone upscale,
Adding landscaping to their roost.

From his Adirondack chair
On his deck, my father
Notices the female in the nest
Raising her wings above her chicks
And the male perched firmly outside the nest

And very likely noticing Dad right back.

Mom is inside with the grandsons
Playing poker.

Off goes the male to hunt
And back he comes to feed his brood.
All day.

"She's the boss," Dad says,
Nodding to the nest.

"She's the boss," the osprey calls right back

As Mom cleans up at the kitchen table.

Morning Meditation

Stepping onto soft, early-morning earth,
My sure right foot descends from the boardwalk
Spanning a spring stream to land just where it
Landed yesterday. Same goes with each move
Around new life rising to the sun
Morning after morning: I mark this ground
In the same way, in the same safe places.

Here, though, a deer has crossed the same soft path;
Each cloven hoof marks a clear signature
Claiming the story of quiet woodlands.
We change the landscape by moving through it:
Walking, touching, breathing, seeing, knowing.

Say: The earth is mine, and I am the earth's.
Moving from step to step, we find the next step

Drifting Off

The dogs
Curl their bodies
Tight against
The strangely mild winds
And a waning moon
That robbed them
Of sleep all week
As it called them
To the edge of my bed,
Alert, upright,
Ready to howl
To their brothers and sisters
The fact of their being
Right here and now.

I have not slept, either.
I am ready for the song,
Ready to be here now,

To trade darkness for a star.

I Am Not Here

My Child,

Tonight I read The Odyssey--
Book 11--
That trip to Hades
Some call hell
And I almost wept
For Odysseus
When he asked
His mother
Why he could not hug her
After not one but three attempts
And she said,
Basically,
Darling son, I am not here.
Where imagination meets spirit,
You are alone.
Your flesh feels it; your mind knows it:
My voice comes from your heart.
All that sacrificing,
Carving up those beautiful animals
For the gods and for your feast
And all that drinking of the blood of your victims
So that I might speak--
What do you think that is about?
Despite all your hard living, you cannot answer.
I will tell you:
It is in your living that you hear my voice;

Take life in your two hands,
But be ready to let it go,
To turn back from everything you think you want
And remember what you love.

Go back, my dear.
Love who you love.
Forget this illusion.

I am not here.

Water

Water
Finds its own level
Is the great leveler

Over time

Reducing everything
To elements
Carrying everything
To the one sea

Primordial chaos
The beginning

With life-giving light
The swirling mass

Of possibility.

Six Yellow Roses

Six yellow roses in a water glass
Are my company tonight.

They are enough
Even if I bought them
For myself,
Which I did
Because they were there and I wanted them.

They will die in a week,
But in the meantime, they will blossom;
I have willed this,

Cutting off their leaves
Trimming their stems
Adding that white powder to the water
And turning up the heat in the house.

I bled when I gripped their stems
To cut all six in one go
Because I do things like that
In a rush and without thinking
Because I see the possibilities and find them
beautiful.

My blood made no difference, and it was a small
price.
In the morning, their fragrance will fill the room.

The flowers will open; their stems will remain strong.

It is not yet over for these roses.

But when it is,
I will invert them until they are dry

And I will remember:
I bought myself roses
Because I wanted them
And I could.

Poseidon's Horses

You watch them canter to shore
In time with the pulse of the sea
Their eager heads down
Their manes white with moist light--
Diamonds cut from the air of morning.

You wait for the thunder
Of their hooves on dry land--
Even the soft sand
Of this beach--

But the horses turn and return
By some miracle you can't name
To the dark waters
And Poseidon.

This time and place--a point of return,
From the the sun and light
To the water that sustains you.

It is a dream.
It is everything,
And you are a bystander.

It is your life.

Return when you want,
A wild horse caressed
In the morning light
And welcome.

This is life, and

It is your dream.